WHITE DOLPHIN

Contents

A Letter from Gill Lewis	3
Judging a Book by its Cover	4
Kara – Inside Out	5
Setting Sail	6–7
Dolphin Experts	8–9
Water Worlds	10
A Good Catch?	11
The Writer's Craft	12–13
Finding Poetry	14
Mystery	15
Pathways… to Another Good Read	16

OXFORD
UNIVERSITY PRESS

Great Clarendon Street, Oxford OX2 6DP

Oxford University Press is a department of the University of Oxford.
It furthers the University's objective of excellence in research,
scholarship, and education by publishing worldwide in

Oxford New York

Auckland Cape Town Dar es Salaam Hong Kong Karachi
Kuala Lumpur Madrid Melbourne Mexico City Nairobi
New Delhi Shanghai Taipei Toronto

With offices in

Argentina Austria Brazil Chile Czech Republic France Greece
Guatemala Hungary Italy Japan South Korea Poland Portugal
Singapore Switzerland Thailand Turkey Ukraine Vietnam

Oxford is a registered trade mark of Oxford University Press in the UK
and in certain other countries

© Oxford University Press 2013

Database right Oxford University Press (maker)

First published 2013

All rights reserved. No part of this publication may be reproduced,
stored in a retrieval system, or transmitted in any form or by any
means, without the prior permission in writing of Oxford University
Press, or as expressly permitted by law, or under terms agreed with
the appropriate reprographics rights organization. Enquiries
concerning reproduction outside the scope of the above should be
sent to the Rights Department, Oxford University Press, at the
address above.

You must not circulate this book in any other binding or cover and you
must impose this same condition on any acquirer.

British Library Cataloguing in Publication Data

Data available

ISBN 978-019-839099-2

10 9 8 7 6 5 4 3 2 1

Printed in China by Printplus

Acknowledgements

The publisher and author would like to thank the following for
their permission to reproduce photographs and other copyright
material:

cover: Eric Gevaert/Alamy & Mark Conlin/Alamy; p3: Gill Lewis; p4
(l, m, r): Oxford University Press; p6: 19th era/Alamy; p12: Gill Lewis

We are grateful for permission to reprint the following copyright
material in this guide:

Gill Lewis: extracts from *White Dolphin* (OUP, 2012), copyright © Gill
Lewis 2012, reprinted by permission of Oxford University Press;
author's sketches, photographs and letter included by permission
of the author.

Extract from report: 'Dolphins save swimmers from Shark',
CBC News, 24.11.2004, reprinted by permission of the Canadian
Broadcasting Corporation.

Encyclopedia entry for 'Cuttlefish' from *World Encyclopedia* (OUP,
2005), reprinted by permission of Oxford University Press.

We have tried to trace and contact all copyright holders before
publication. If notified, the publishers will be pleased to rectify any
errors or omissions at the earliest opportunity.

Illustrations by Steve Evans.

A Letter from Gill Lewis

Dear Reader,

Some stories arrive in a flash of inspiration, but more often than not, the idea begins slowly, whirling around in the mind, gathering speed and momentum. Although *White Dolphin* took about nine months to write, it began many years ago, when I was ten. I remember sitting on the side of my father's small boat, looking down at my reflection in the water. It was early morning on the Loughor Estuary, South Wales. A thin sea mist lay above the water. The air was still. The sea was flat, like glass. The silence was broken by the sound of dolphin breaths bursting above the surface. A pod of dolphins rose up from another world, it seemed, to spend some time with us. One dolphin turned on its side to look at me and I looked back into its small eye, each of us curious about the other. That moment of connection, at the interface of our different worlds, has always stayed with me.

It was this connection between a girl and a dolphin that I wanted to write about. *White Dolphin* started out as a story for much younger readers, about a girl who could talk with dolphins through understanding their clicks and whistles. However, the more I researched about dolphins, I began to realize that a more powerful story could be told through keeping the dolphin true to its own nature.

My research led me beneath the waves to discover the incredible sea life we have around our British coasts and also the threats facing vulnerable habitats. Much of my research was based upon the Lyme Bay Reefs project, where the Devon Wildlife Trust has been studying the reefs for nearly twenty years and has been campaigning for their protection from damaging fishing practices, specifically commercial scallop dredging. The underlying story in *White Dolphin* became a story about the need to protect our oceans for the future of our wildlife and also for the sustainability of fishing for our future.

But stories need characters and a heart, and so *White Dolphin* became Kara's story, about a girl who is desperately searching for the truth behind the disappearance of her mother. It became a story about friendship and hope, and about finding the courage to fight for what you believe.

I hope you enjoy *White Dolphin*.

Gill Lewis

Judging a Book by its Cover

A book cover gives us an impression of what a book is about. Here are three covers for *White Dolphin*.

A

B

C

With a partner, talk about which one you prefer and why. What do the different covers tell us about the story inside?

Designer choices

Designers have to make many decisions when creating a new cover. Make notes about some of the choices made by the designers of these covers by copying and completing the table below.

	Cover A	Cover B	Cover C
Title (e.g. font, size, position)			
Images (e.g. impact, size, position)			
Other text (e.g. content, position)			

Create a new design for *White Dolphin* or another book you know well. Be prepared to explain your design choices.

Kara – Inside Out

White Dolphin is written from Kara's point of view. This means we gain a good idea of her thoughts, her hopes and her fears.

Floating in the seaweed are words which describe some of the things she feels and thinks. See if you can untangle the letters into words.

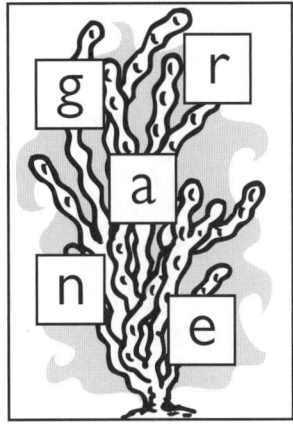 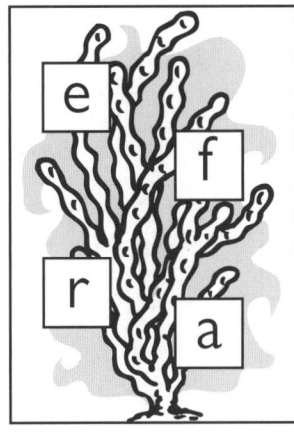 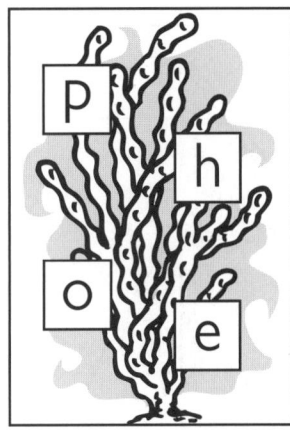 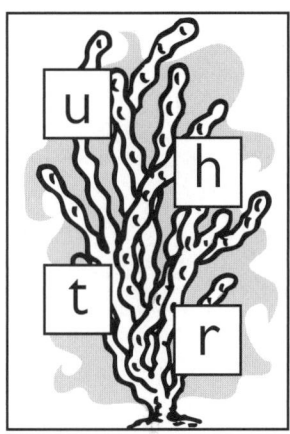

1 _____   2 _____   3 _____   4 _____

Character profile

Create your own character outline, like the one here, but larger. As you read the story, note down how Kara is feeling inside (inside the profile) and link it to how she shows her feelings (outside the profile).

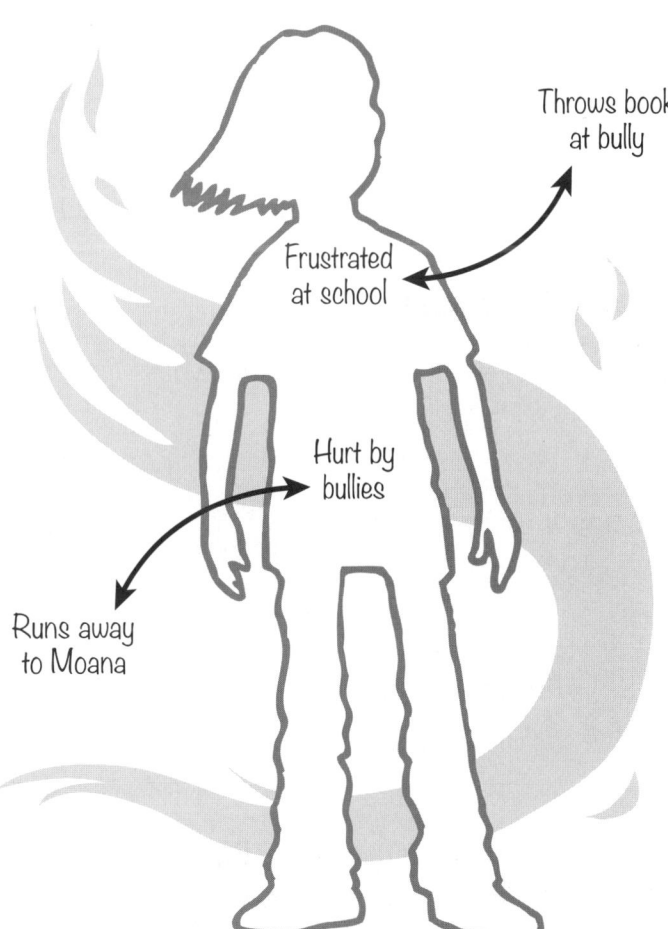

Answers

1 anger, 2 fear, 3 hope, 4 hurt

Setting Sail

The *Moana* is important to Kara and sailing is a significant part of her life.

In the story, you will read some specialist terms relating to sailing boats. See how well you know the parts of a sailing boat, by matching the labels to the diagram.

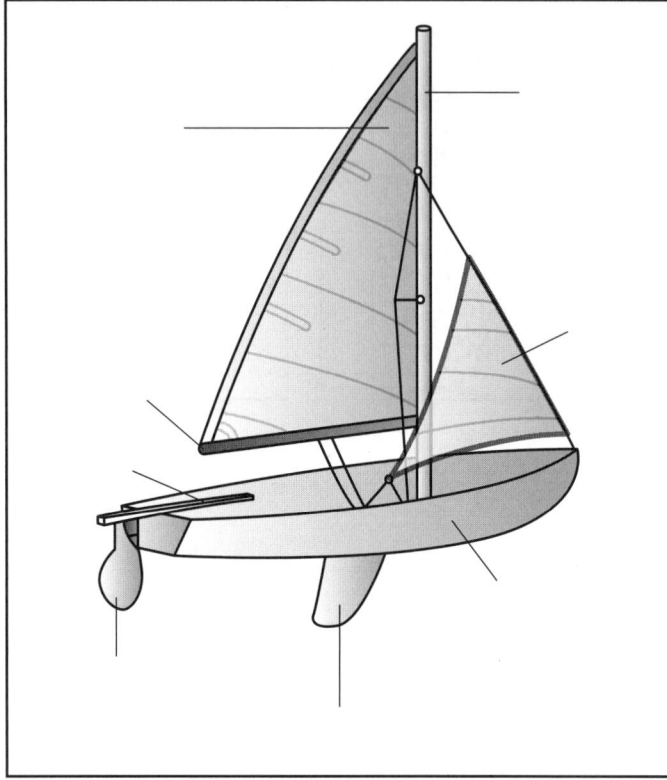

boom – the pole attached to the bottom of the mainsail

hull – the body or shell of the boat

jib – the smaller sail that provides extra wind power

keel – the fin that sticks out of the bottom of the boat and helps to provide balance

mainsail – the larger sail that catches the wind to provide power

mast – the large upright pole to which the sail is attached

rudder – a sort of paddle that sticks down in the water and helps the boat to steer

tiller – the handle attached to the rudder, used by the sailor to steer the boat

Find out about...

Do some research about sailing boats and write up your findings. Here are some ideas:

Write a glossary of technical language relating to boats (e.g. port, starboard, aft).

Find out about different types of sailing boats, e.g. sloop, ketch, schooner.

Research one or more famous sailing ships (e.g. the *Mary Rose*, the *Beagle*).

Find out about how to sail a boat (e.g. explain tacking).

Setting Sail

A wonderful boat

Think about how these extracts make *Moana* seem special and different.

> 'With her terracotta sails and open wooden deck, she stands out from the moulded whiteness of the modern yachts.'

> 'She could have sailed out from one of the old photos of this harbour a hundred years ago.'

> 'There's real craftsmanship there.'

Complete one of the following activities:

- Design the advertisement, written by Kara's father, to sell *Moana*.
- Imagine that Kara gives a talk in class about why *Moana* is special to her. Plan and deliver the talk that she gives.
- Create some of the documents that Kara's dad keeps in the folder on *Moana* (see Chapter 10 of the story). The documents should detail her restoration and return to sailing.

Sailing expressions

In everyday talk, we use expressions derived from sailing. Here are some of them. Discuss how they might apply to characters in the story.

Expression	Meaning
to sail against the wind	to oppose popular ideas or opinions
to sail close to the wind	to act on the boundary of what is right and proper
to take the wind out of someone's sails	to get ahead of and frustrate someone
to sail into someone or something	to attack them/it with force

WHITE DOLPHIN

Dolphin Experts

Kara and her friends at Marine Life Rescue know a lot about dolphins. How much do you know?

Use the information from the story (in particular, Chapters 16–20 and 24), together with the fact files on this page, to help you answer the questions in this quiz.

Dolphin quiz

1. Dolphins breathe through their mouths. True or false?
2. What is a young dolphin called?
3. A dolphin will die if it goes completely to sleep. True or false?
4. Dolphins eat only seaweed. True or false?
5. What is the proper name for a dolphin's snout?
6. List at least three ways in which dolphins communicate.
7. Pectoral fins are part of the tail. True or false?
8. What is the collective noun for a group of dolphins?

Fact File 1

Dolphin communication

Dolphins can communicate in lots of ways, including:

- vocally, through whistles and clicking noises
- tail slaps
- jaw claps
- 'chuffs' (breathing out loudly)
- gestures (e.g. shaking head, opening mouth)
- releasing bubbles.

Fact File 2

Parts of a dolphin

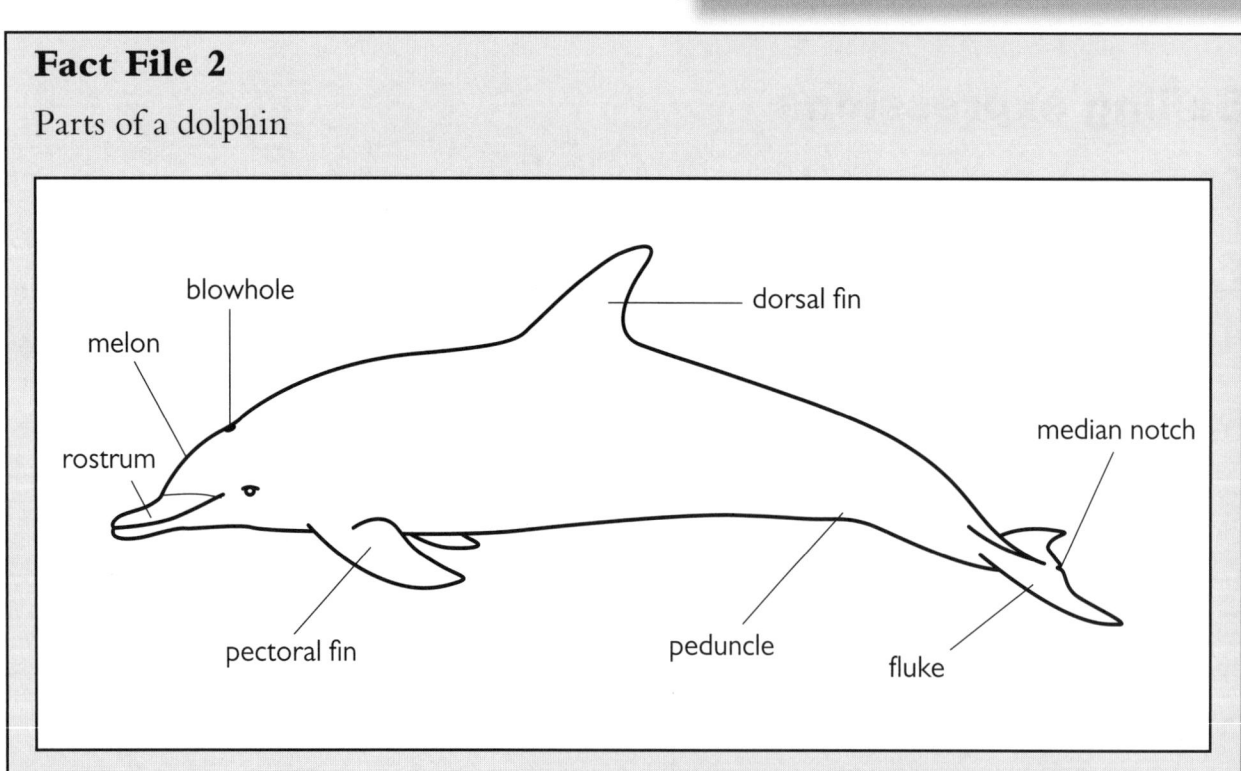

Dolphin Experts

Dolphin heroes

There are many stories of dolphins helping humans. Here is one such news story. Unfortunately, it has been jumbled up. See if you can put it into the right order.

Dolphins save swimmers from shark
November 24, 2004

A About halfway through the swim, a pod of dolphins 'came steaming at us' and started circling, startling the swimmers, he said. Howes said he was unnerved by the speed of the approach, thinking perhaps it was a group of aggressive males or dolphins protecting their baby.

B The shark left as a rescue boat neared, but the dolphins remained close by as the group swam back to shore.

C The dolphins bunched the four swimmers together by circling about 4 metres from them, and slapping the water with their tails for about 40 minutes. Howes said he drifted away from the main group when an opening occurred. One large dolphin became agitated and submerged toward Howes, who turned to see where it would surface.

D A group of lifeguards swimming off the coast of New Zealand may have been saved from a shark attack recently by several protective dolphins that helped to hold the predator at bay. Lifeguard Rob Howes said he and three female lifeguards were on a training swim about 100 metres off Ocean Beach near Whangarei on the North Island.

E That, he says, is when he saw a great white shark about two metres away in the beach's crystal clear waters. 'The form came and travelled in an arc around me. I knew instinctively what it was,' he said.

F When the shark started moving toward the women, including his 15-year-old daughter, the dolphins 'went into hyperdrive', said Howes. 'I would suggest they were creating a confusion screen around the girls. It was just a mass of fins, backs and human heads.'

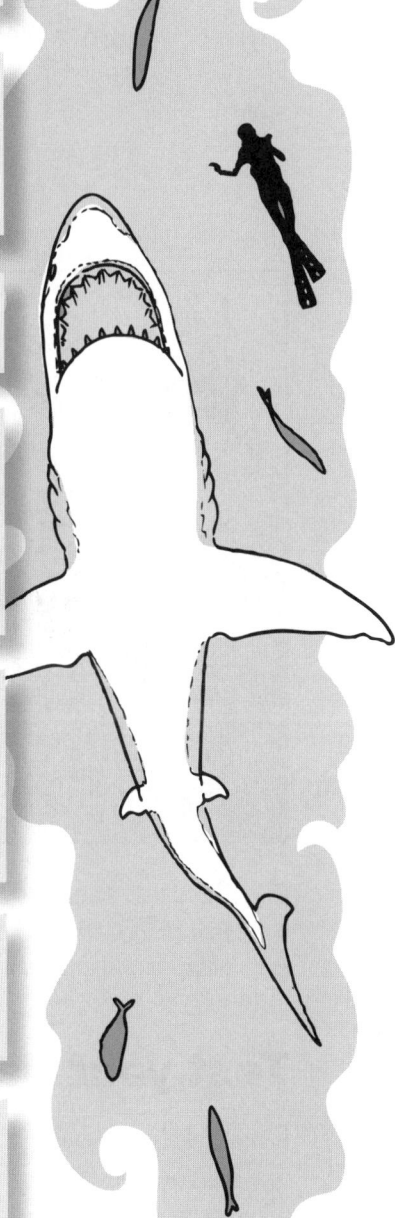

Answers

D, A, C, E, F, B

WHITE DOLPHIN

Water Worlds

Gill Lewis gives us a glimpse of a strange and beautiful world beneath the waves. Look at some of her descriptions of plants and creatures that live in the sea.

'rocks jewelled with pink and green anemones'

'feather-stars and sea-fans'

'soft pink corals and yellow sponges'

'a purple sea-slug threads its way through reddish seaweed'

'A velvet swimming crab scuttles by'

- Research the wonderful plants and creatures living around the British coastline.
- Make a collage of names and pictures to illustrate the variety.

Test your design skills!

Design a theme park, based on the beautiful and fantastical world under the waves. Your design might include:

- the name of the park
- an overall map/plan
- explanations of rides
- descriptions of facilities (e.g. cafes, shops, information points)
- promotional material (e.g. leaflets).

WHITE DOLPHIN

A Good Catch?

Humans have a big influence over life in the seas and oceans. Fishing has a huge impact.

Fishing is an important industry in Cornwall, where the story is set. It provides a livelihood for many people, but there are also issues with fishing in a responsible way.

There are lots of ways to catch different types of fish and seafood. Here are some of them.

◎ Choose the right description to match to each picture.

A) Drift nets are suspended in the sea, to drift with the current. The mesh of the nets is designed to catch fish as they swim through. Marine mammals can become entangled in the nets and drown.

B) Dredging takes shellfish such as oysters and scallops from the seabed. A dredge is a metal-framed basket with a raking bar attached to it. As the dredge is pulled over the seabed, the raking bar dislodges shellfish into the basket.

C) Pelagic trawling involves pulling nets through the water in order to catch shoals of fish. Sometimes a pair of trawlers pulls huge nets to catch fish. Marine mammals can get caught up in the nets.

D) Pots or creels are left on the seabed to trap creatures such as crabs and lobsters. They capture live animals, which can be returned to the sea if necessary.

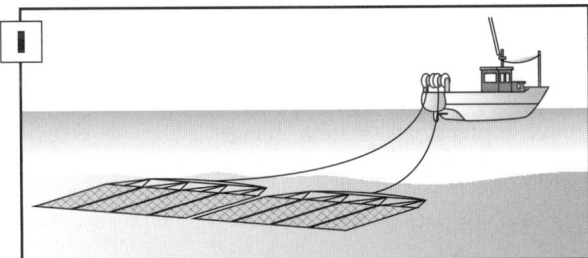

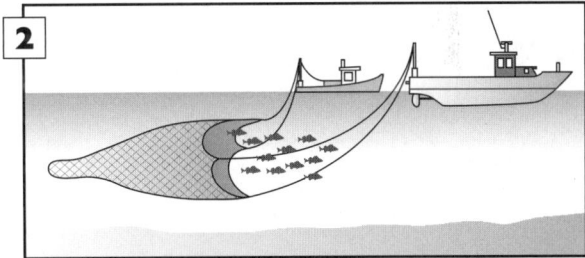

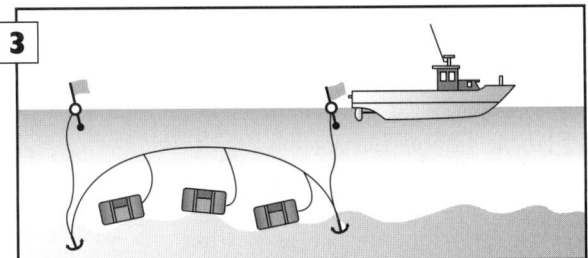

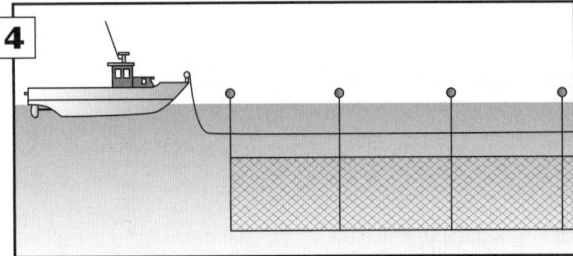

◎ Discuss the issues and dangers that might be associated with each method.
◎ Find out about other fishing methods and discuss which methods are safest for the marine environment.

Answers
A4, B1, C2, D3

WHITE DOLPHIN

The Writer's Craft

Researching a story

Writers often research the subjects they write about. Think about what subjects Gill Lewis will have researched for this story (e.g. dolphins, fishing).

As you can see from this page, Gill finds interesting ways to research her stories.

Gill taking a boat to see dolphins

'I collect pieces of driftwood and take them home and paint seascapes in acrylic. It feels as if a piece of the storm that brought the wood on the shore is within the wood.'

A painting of the sea on a piece of driftwood collected by Gill

A photo of dolphins that Gill took while out on a boat trip in Pembrokeshire

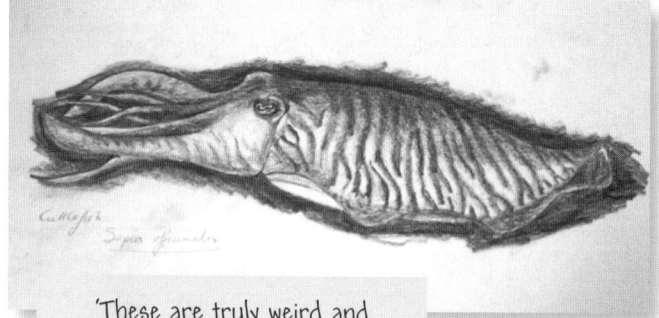

'These are truly weird and amazing creatures, able to change colour, shape and texture to blend in with any background. They are fearsome hunters too.'

A sketch of a cuttlefish that Gill created when imagining the setting for White Dolphin

Research ideas

Choose one of the following story ideas for Gill's next book. Suggest ways she might research the story.

- A story set in a circus (e.g. visiting a circus, sketching circus acts, collecting circus flyers, exploring the websites of world circuses such as the Cirque du Soleil and the Chinese State Circus)
- A story about Roman Britain
- A story about skydiving
- A story about a young athlete
- A story about a human base on Mars

The Writer's Craft

Stealth killers

Once a writer has completed their research, they need to turn it into a piece of entertaining writing.

Read these two texts about cuttlefish. One is from an encyclopedia and the other is from *White Dolphin*.

cuttlefish

Cephalopod mollusc related to the squid and octopus. Like squid, cuttlefish swim rapidly by the propulsion of a jet of water forced out through a siphon. They have ten sucker-covered arms on the head, two much longer than the rest. Their flattened bodies contain the familiar chalky cuttle-bone. Capable of rapid colour changes, they can also eject blue-black 'ink' as a means of protection. Family Sepiidae; species Sepia officinalis.

Its camouflage is far too good. But then I see it watching me from the sand below me. Only the horseshoe-shaped black pupils of its eyes give it away. The speckled pattern of its body perfectly matches the sand beneath. I reach out to touch it, but it rises upwards, away from me, and stops mid-water, changing colour in an instant to bright red. It looks like a small deflated beach ball with long tentacles at one end. Its body is fringed by a rim of fins that ripple along each side. The tentacles stick out straight in front of it, like a sword.

With a partner, talk about:
◎ the different purposes of the two texts
◎ the language techniques and style used by each writer (e.g. the use of similes, descriptive language, the precise language used when giving facts, etc.)

Find an encyclopedia description of another sea creature that Kara and Felix might see as they swim, for example:
◎ basking shark
◎ octopus
◎ starfish
◎ seahorse
◎ ray.

Write a short, extra episode to the story, including your chosen sea creature.

Finding Poetry

You can find poetry in the words of other writers. Look at the poetry of Gill Lewis's words.

The poems on this page are made of words found in her story. Read the poems and then look at where in the story the words have come from. Discuss the techniques used to create the poems.

Moana

The sea is alive in the bay,
And it is just us again,
Moana, Dad and me.
The ocean rushes beneath us.
Waves slap against Moana's hull,
Like a heartbeat.
If I close my eyes
I see Dad steaming curved planks of wood,
Mum laying white caulk between the boards,
And me sitting in the dirt.
Mum, Dad and me.

(from Chapter 3)

Beached

White dolphin lying on the shore
Small waves run in and furl around her
The sand is wet and hard

White dolphin lying on the shore
Seaweed curls around her tail flukes
The tide is ebbing out to sea

White dolphin lying on the shore
Her eye is partly open
She doesn't blink or move

White dolphin lying on the shore
Mesh nylon wrapped so tightly
Cut into her dolphin smile

I don't want to be here any more.

(from Chapter 16)

The Seal

His big dog eyes
are chocolate brown.
He snorts a breath.
Silver bubbles
spiral upwards,
and he twists away,
flippers pressed together,
his grey body sliding through the water.
And we're twisting through the water too
down
      down
            down.

(from Chapter 28)

There are lots of ways to find poems in other people's writing. Have a go at writing your own poem, using some of the words of *White Dolphin*.

Mystery

There is a mystery at the heart of this story – what has happened to Kara's mum? What do these extracts tell us about Kara's mum?

'She sent a sign. I saw a dolphin, a white dolphin. Mum sent it for us.'

'Kay should never have left. Her responsibilities were *here*.'

'Mum's a marine biologist... She stops people catching wild dolphins.'

'She never kept *things*. She didn't even want a wedding ring from Dad.'

Missing person

Imagine you are part of the team of detectives investigating her disappearance. Copy and complete these case notes. Discuss what you think may have happened to her and put this in your conclusions.

Missing Person Report	
Picture	**Personal details** Name: Kay Wood Age: Address: Nationality: Marital status: Children:
Occupation	
Interests	
Last known movements	
Conclusions	

WHITE DOLPHIN

Pathways... to Another Good Read

Other books about animals

Sky Hawk by Gill Lewis
ISBN 978 0 19 913719 0
When Callum finds Iona fishing by a loch on his family farm he asks her to leave, but Iona has a secret. She shares the secret with Callum and so begins a deep friendship, which turns into a wildlife rescue mission that will change their lives forever.

Eye of the Wolf by Daniel Pennac
ISBN 978 14 0 632273 6
A wolf from Alaska and a boy from Africa share an extraordinary bond when they confront each other across a zoo enclosure.

The Last Wolf by Michael Morpurgo
ISBN 978 0 19 832983 1
When Robbie McLeod finds an orphaned wolf cub and vows to take care of him, it is the beginning of an adventure that sweeps them from the Highlands of Scotland to the high seas and beyond.

War Horse by Michael Morpurgo
ISBN 978 14 0 522666 0
This is the story of a powerful friendship between a horse, Joey, and a young soldier during the First World War. The story has also been adapted into a play, first performed at the National Theatre with life-size puppets taking the roles of the horses, and a film.

Fire, Bed and Bone by Henrietta Branford
ISBN 978 0 19 832859 9
The year is 1381. Rebellion is brewing, and life for man – and dog – is about to change dramatically… Told through the eyes of a hunting dog, *Fire, Bed and Bone* is an unusual and engaging look at an important time in British history.

Dog Finds Lost Dolphins! And More True Stories of Amazing Animal Heroes (National Geographic Kids)
ISBN 978 14 2 631031 7
A fascinating non-fiction book containing true stories about some wonderful animals, including photographs and amazing facts.

Other books about loss, friendship and growing up

My Sister Lives on the Mantelpiece by Annabel Pitcher
ISBN 978 0 19 913728 2
It's been five years since Jamie's sister Rose was blown up by a terrorist bomb. The grief has torn his family apart – his mum has gone and his dad barely notices him. But Jamie hardly remembers Rose. He's more interested in his cat Roger and in keeping his new friend Sunya secret from his father. Jamie longs for his mother to come home, but will he ever get the fresh start he longs for?

A Monster Calls by Patrick Ness
ISBN 978 1 40 633934 5
'The monster showed up after midnight. As they do.' But it isn't the monster Conor's been expecting… the one he's had nearly every night since his mother started her treatments… This monster is different. It wants the most dangerous thing of all from Conor. It wants the truth. A moving tale of love, loss and hope through the eyes of a young boy.

Starseeker by Tim Bowler
ISBN 978 0 19 832890 2
Luke is still coming to terms with the death of his father, when he finds himself the target of a notorious gang at his school. He has a choice: join them by breaking into a house to prove his worth or stand up to them and become their latest victim. Skin, the leader of the gang, is violent and unforgiving, but Luke is willing to risk everything to protect a precious secret.

Ostrich Boys by Keith Gray
ISBN 978 0 09 945657 5
Kenny, Sim and Blake embark on a remarkable journey – taking the ashes of their best friend Ross to the hamlet of Ross in Scotland. After a dispiriting funeral, they feel that taking Ross to Ross will be a fitting memorial for a boy who changed all their lives through friendship. Little do they realize how much Ross can still affect them.

WHITE DOLPHIN